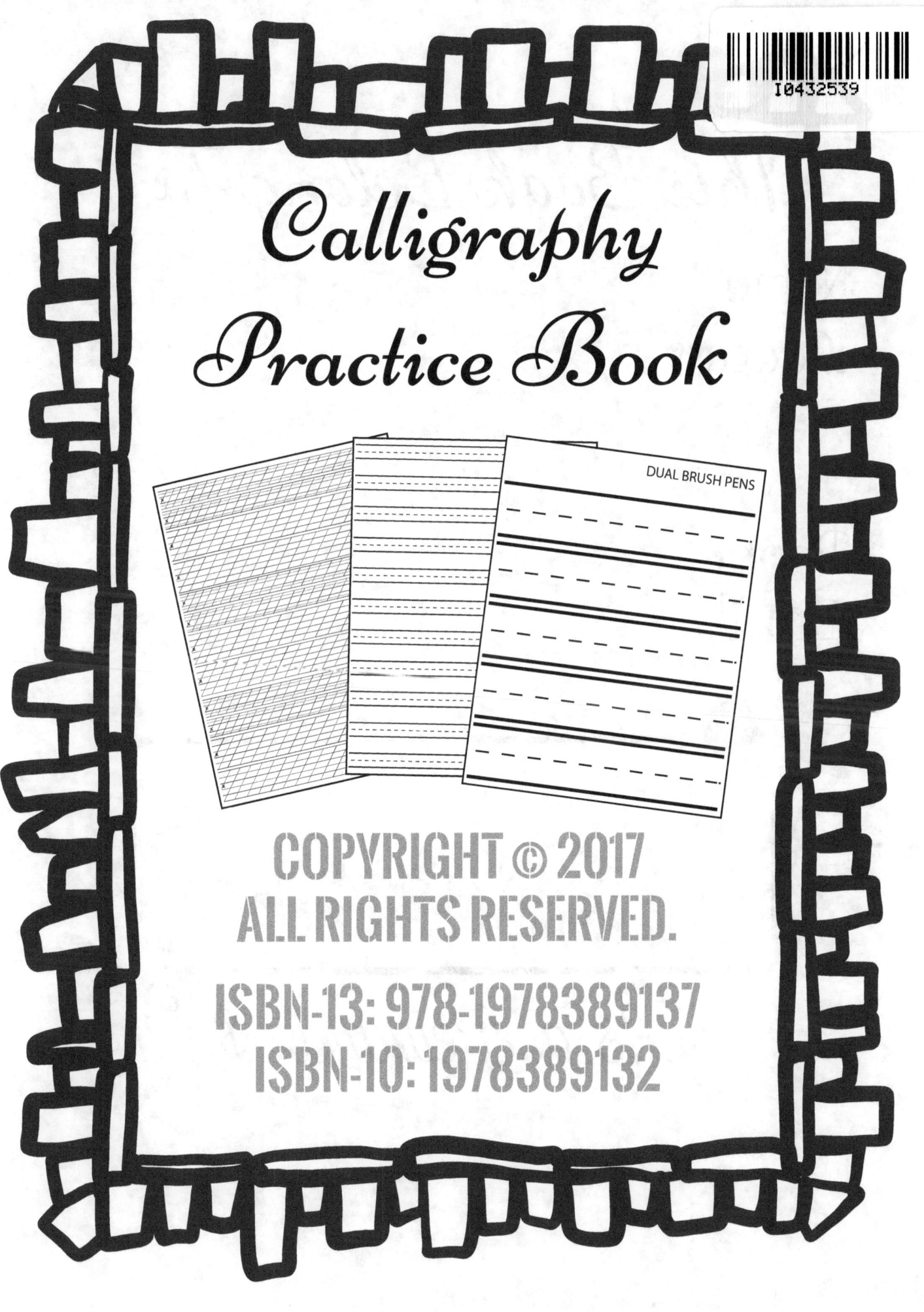

This Book Belong To:

Name _____

Address _____
_____
_____

Phone _____

Email _____

" _____ "

As a Reward: $ _____

Table of Contents

Section 1
Angled Line

Section 2
Straight Line

Section 3
Dual Brush Pens

DUAL BRUSH PENS

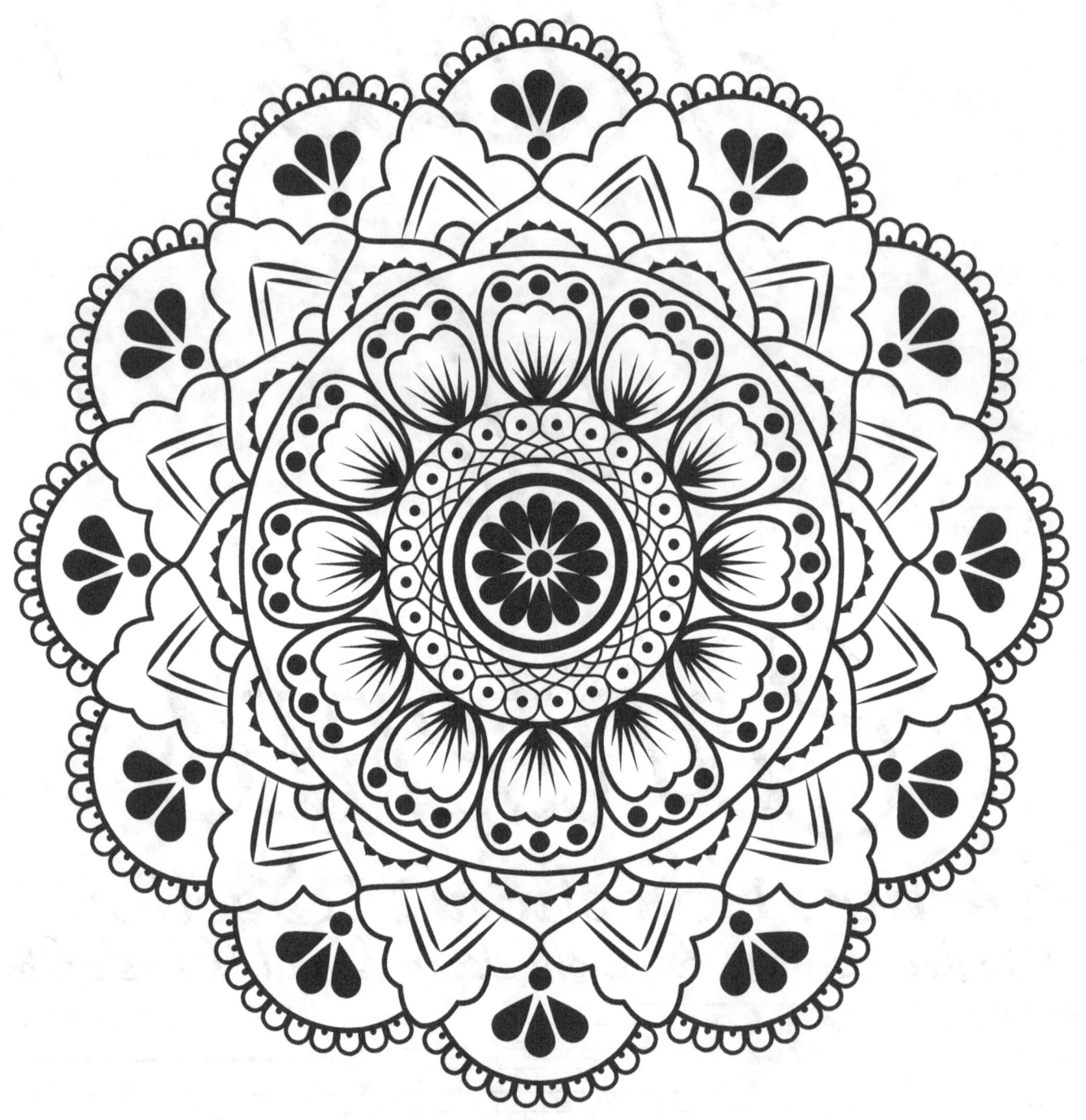

Section 1
Angled Line

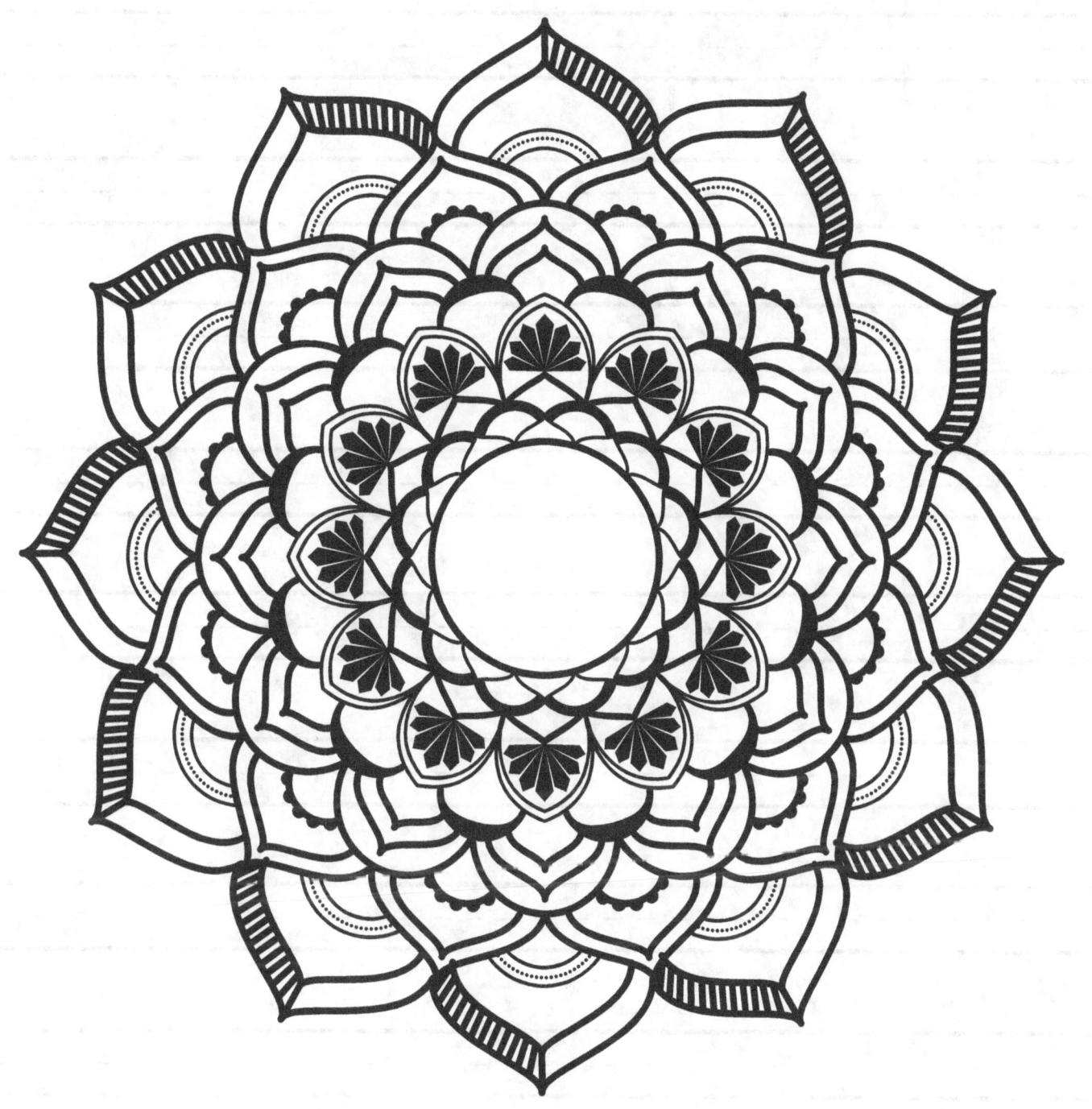

Section 2
Straight Line

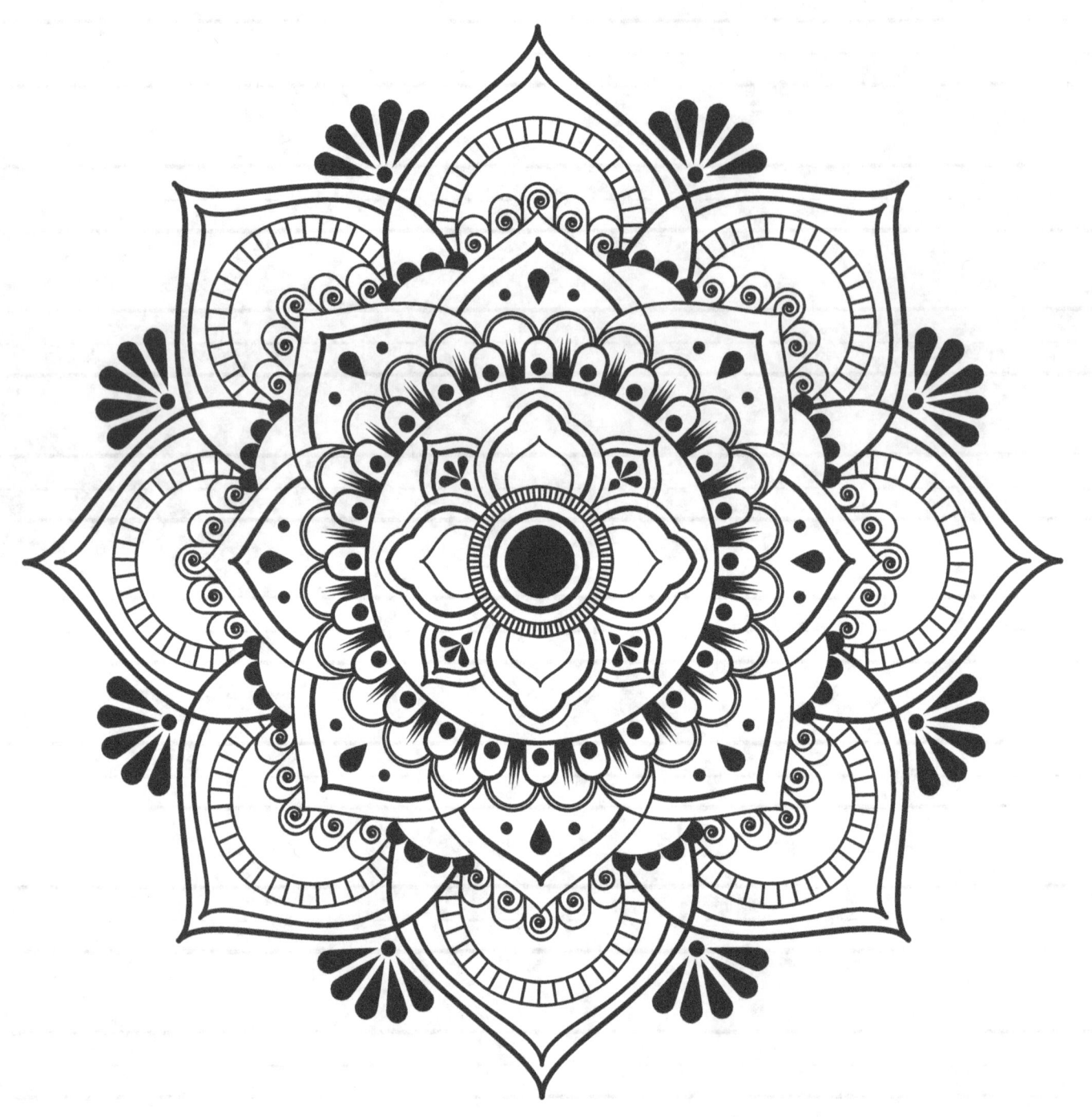

Section 3
Dual Brush Pens

DUAL BRUSH PENS

DUAL BRUSH PENS

DUAL BRUSH PENS

DUAL BRUSH PENS

DUAL BRUSH PENS

DUAL BRUSH PENS

DUAL BRUSH PENS

DUAL BRUSH PENS

DUAL BRUSH PENS

DUAL BRUSH PENS

DUAL BRUSH PENS

DUAL BRUSH PENS

DUAL BRUSH PENS

DUAL BRUSH PENS

DUAL BRUSH PENS

DUAL BRUSH PENS

DUAL BRUSH PENS

DUAL BRUSH PENS

DUAL BRUSH PENS

DUAL BRUSH PENS

DUAL BRUSH PENS

DUAL BRUSH PENS

DUAL BRUSH PENS

DUAL BRUSH PENS

DUAL BRUSH PENS

DUAL BRUSH PENS

DUAL BRUSH PENS

DUAL BRUSH PENS

DUAL BRUSH PENS

DUAL BRUSH PENS

DUAL BRUSH PENS

DUAL BRUSH PENS

DUAL BRUSH PENS

DUAL BRUSH PENS

DUAL BRUSH PENS

DUAL BRUSH PENS

DUAL BRUSH PENS

DUAL BRUSH PENS

DUAL BRUSH PENS

DUAL BRUSH PENS

www.ingramcontent.com/pod-product-compliance
Lightning Source LLC
Chambersburg PA
CBHW082337220526
45470CB00008B/2547